You Laugh You Lose Challenge Joke Book- 7, 8 & 9 Year Old Edition

The LOL Interactive Joke and Riddle Book Contest Game for Boys and Girls Age 7 to 9

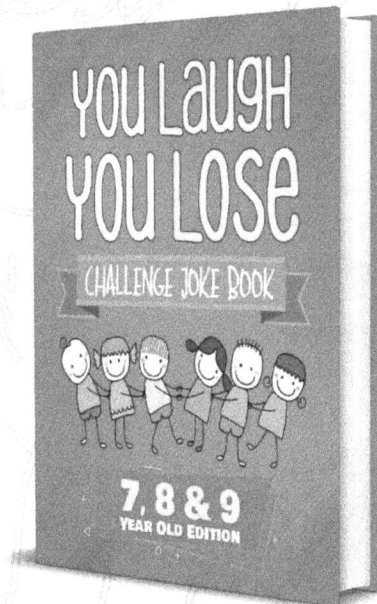

Natalie Fleming

DEDICATION

This book is dedicated to all the wonderful kids around who make us learn every day.

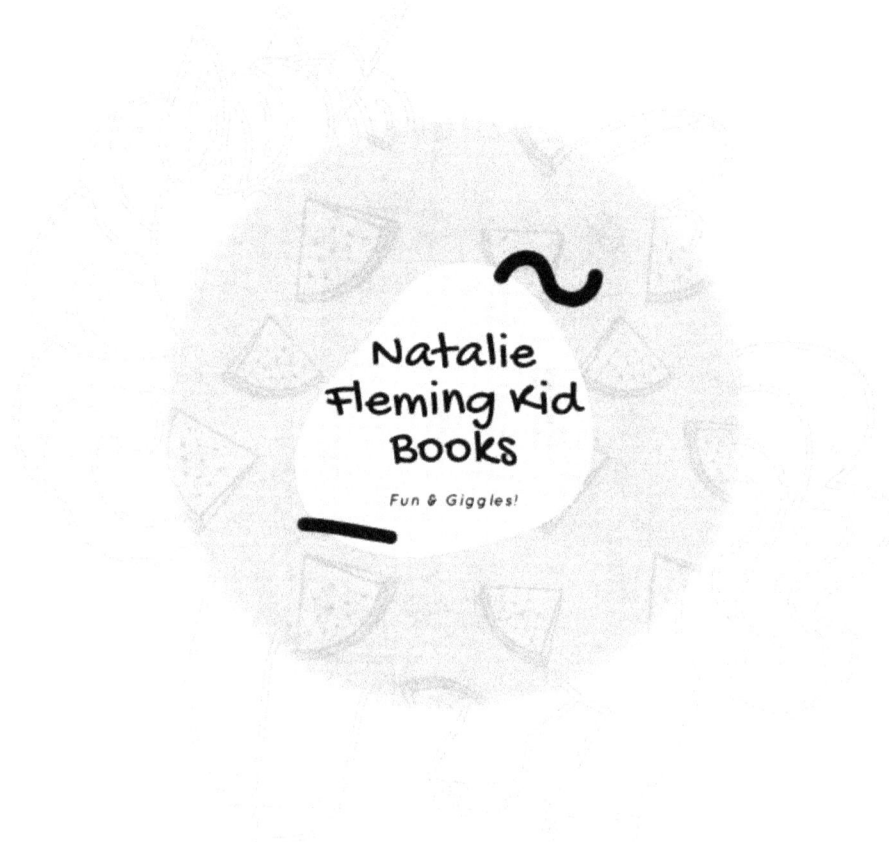

Natalie
Fleming Kid
Books

Fun & Giggles!

Welcome!

Hi There,

This is my new book for kids, and I am very excited to share the content with you. You can check all my books by visiting the Author Profile.

As a token of appreciation, I wish to share some Fun Slime Recipes with you.

Either Click Here

Or copy/type

http://eepurl.com/dtOspz

I would be sharing the new updates with you in the coming months.

Cheers!

Natalie Fleming

Rules

So let the games begin!

Below are the rules.

- Divide yourselves into two teams :
  Team Unicorn & Team Mermaid

- The game is divided into four sections:

  - *Jokes*

  -- *Riddles*

  - *Who am I*

  - *Knock Knock Jokes*

- Each page would have points for the other team

- Add the points at the end of each section

- Finally, add the points of all the sections

- The team with more point is the winner

Team Details

Divide the team equally (1,2 or 3 members each)

- ## *Team Unicorn :*

Write your names ....

- ## *Team Mermaid :*

Write your names ....

- ## *The Umpire:* *Let your parents, elder brother-sister, or friend decide in case there is any confusion/dispute in each game*

Name of the Umpire...

Game 1: Jokes
You Laugh You Lose

- Each team would get two jokes at a time.

- If the other team member laughs at the joke, 1 point is given to the first team (team reading the joke).

- Add the points at the end of the chapter.

- Let the Umpire decide in case there is any confusion in whether the other team laughed or not. *(A smile is also considered for a point!)*

Let's start with jokes, control your laughter to win! He He!

Joke Round 1:Team Unicorn:

(It's your turn to read the jokes)

> ### 1. Why are all numbers afraid of 7?
>
> *Because 78 (ate) 9*

> ### 2. How to make a lemon drop?
>
> *Throw it down*

** How many times did the other team member laughed, once or twice, add your points!!

<u>Team Unicorn Points:</u> ……../02

Joke Round 1: Team Mermaid:

(It's your turn to read the jokes)

3. Why is duck considered wise?

Wise Quacker

4. How to talk to Monsters?

Using Big words

** How many times did the other team member laughed, once or twice, add your points!!

Team Mermaid Points: ……../02

Joke Round 2:Team Unicorn:
(It's your turn to read the jokes)

5. Which building in London has maximum stories?

Library

6. Why is ocean considered friendly?

They always wave

** *How many times did the other team member laughed, once or twice, add your points!!*

Team Unicorn Points: ..../02

Joke Round 2:Team Mermaid:
(It's your turn to read the jokes)

7. Which mouth freshener do scientists use?

Experi - mints!

8. Which is the most talkative flower?

Tulip (2 Lip)

** How many times did the other team member laughed, once or twice, add your points!!

Team Mermaid Points: ……../02

Joke Round 3:Team Unicorn:

(It's your turn to read the jokes)

9. Nobody is afraid of this Lion?

Dandelion (A Flower)

10. The funny mountain's name was?

Hill-arious

** How many times did the other team member laughed, once or twice, add your points!!

Team Unicorn Points: ..../02

Joke Round 3:Team Mermaid:
(It's your turn to read the jokes)

11. Why did Matt throw the clock out of the window?

He wanted to see time fly

12. What did Snowman do at the weekend?

Chill Out

** How many times did the other team member laughed, once or twice, add your points!!

Team Mermaid Points: ..../02

Joke Round 4:Team Unicorn:

(It's your turn to read the jokes)

13. Why is balloon afraid of music?

Because it was pop music

14. What do you like to put in the Pie?

Teeth

** *How many times did the other team member laughed, once or twice, add your points!!*

Team Unicorn Points: ..../02

Joke Round 4: Team Mermaid:
(It's your turn to read the jokes)

15. How does the Bus starts?

With a B

16. Which game do Pumpkins play?

Squash

** How many times did the other team member laughed, once or twice, add your points!!

Team Mermaid Points: ..../02

Joke Round 5:Team Unicorn:

(It's your turn to read the jokes)

17. This is a Key with a leg but can't open the door?
Tur-key

18. Which is the loudest pet?
Trum-pet

** How many times did the other team member laughed, once or twice, add your points!!

Team Unicorn Points: ……../02

Joke Round 5:Team Mermaid:
(It's your turn to read the jokes)

19. Why no one trust stairs?

Stairs are always upto something

20. What do you call a Bear with no ear?

B (B-ear)

** How many times did the other team member laughed, once or twice, add your points!!

Team Mermaid Points: ..../02

Joke Round 6:Team Unicorn:

(It's your turn to read the jokes)

21. How does a Cat walk down the highway?

MEEEEOWWWWW

22. Who is the best underwater detective?

James Pond

** How many times did the other team member laughed, once or twice, add your points!!

Team Unicorn Points: ……../02

Joke Round 6:Team Mermaid:

(It's your turn to read the jokes)

23. Which book do eggs read?

Yolk Book

---

24. What time do ducks go for a morning walk?

At a Quack

** How many times did the other team member laughed, once or twice, add your points!!

Team Mermaid Points: ..../02

Joke Round 7:Team Unicorn:

(It's your turn to read the jokes)

25 Why was the deer afraid of the fastest cat?

Because it was a cheetah

26. Why was john running around his bed?

To catch his sleep

** How many times did the other team member laughed, once or twice, add your points!!

Team Unicorn Points: ..../02

Joke Round 7:Team Mermaid:

(It's your turn to read the jokes)

> ### 27. Which is the better hand to write with?
> No hand, write by pen

> ### 28. Why Mickey mouse wanted to go to space?
> To find Pluto

** How many times did the other team member laughed, once or twice, add your points!!

Team Mermaid Points: ……..../02

Joke Round 8: Team Unicorn:
(It's your turn to read the jokes)

29. How is holy water made?

Boil the hell out

30. Why do you think the broom was late?

It overswept

** How many times did the other team member laughed, once or twice, add your points!!

Team Unicorn Points: ..../02

Joke Round 8:Team Mermaid:
(It's your turn to read the jokes)

31. Why were people tired in November?

They just completed 31 days of October

32. A man came on Tuesday and after 2 days left on Tuesday, How?

His horse name was Tuesday

** How many times did the other team member laughed, once or twice, add your points!!

Team Mermaid Points: ……../02

Joke Round 9: Team Unicorn:

(It's your turn to read the jokes)

33. Where do ghosts keep their kids during the day?

Day Scare

34. What is the favorite breakfast dish of witch?

Sandwitch

** *How many times did the other team member laughed, once or twice, add your points!!*

Team Unicorn Points: ..../ 02

Joke Round 9:Team Mermaid:
(It's your turn to read the jokes)

35. Witches sharing room in a hostel are called?

Broom Mates

36. Which is the most expensive soup?

24 carrot (carat) soup

** How many times did the other team member laughed, once or twice, add your points!!

Team Mermaid Points: ……../02

Joke Round 10:Team Unicorn:

(It's your turn to read the jokes)

37. Which tree does chicken come from?

Poul-Tree

38. In which business Frosty was involved?

Snow Business

** How many times did the other team member laughed, once or twice, add your points!!

Team Unicorn Points: ……../02

Joke Round 10:Team Mermaid:
(It's your turn to read the jokes)

39. What do elephants in the forest sing in Christmas?

Jungle Bells Jungle Bells

40. The cat in the sands is called?

Sandy Claws

** How many times did the other team member laughed, once or twice, add your points!!

Team Mermaid Points: ..../02

Joke Round 11:Team Unicorn:

(It's your turn to read the jokes)

41. Why was hot faster than cold?

Because you can catch cold

42. Who can meet black cat and bad luck at once?

Mouse

** How many times did the other team member laughed, once or twice, add your points!!

Team Unicorn Points: ……../02

Joke Round 11:Team Mermaid:
(It's your turn to read the jokes)

43. Where was the dog going in the car?

To the barking lot

44. Why nose hated going to school?

Because it was always picked

** How many times did the other team member laughed, once or twice, add your points!!

Team Mermaid Points: ……../02

Joke Round 12: Team Unicorn:

(It's your turn to read the jokes)

45. Where do Eskimo keep their figs?

figloo

46. Why doesn't Crab share with friends?

Because it is Shell-Fish

** How many times did the other team member laughed, once or twice, add your points!!

Team Unicorn Points: ……../02

Joke Round 12: Team Mermaid:

(It's your turn to read the jokes)

47. Why did the music teacher distributed ladders?

To reach high notes

48. Why were librarians sick?

Due to Bookworms

** How many times did the other team member laughed, once or twice, add your points!!

Team Mermaid Points: ……../02

Joke Round 13: Team Unicorn:

(It's your turn to read the jokes)

49. How did Superman eat his cereals?

In a Superbowl

50. Who is Snailer?

A snail riding a ship

** How many times did the other team member laughed, once or twice, add your points!!

Team Unicorn Points: ..…..../02

Joke Round 13:Team Mermaid:

(It's your turn to read the jokes)

51. What is the frog's favorite snack?

French Flies

52. Which shark delivers gifts during Christmas?

Santa Jaws

** How many times did the other team member laughed, once or twice, add your points!!

Team Mermaid Points: ..../02

Joke Round 14: Team Unicorn:
(It's your turn to read the jokes)

53. Which fruit would you get by hanging iphone on Christmas tree?

Pine (Christmas tree) apple (iphone)

54. He laughs, bring present ,and scratches your furniture?

Santa Claws

** How many times did the other team member laughed, once or twice, add your points!!

Team Unicorn Points: ..../02

Joke Round14: Team Mermaid:

(It's your turn to read the jokes)

55. What did the calculator say to the students?

You can count on me

56. Why Leopards can't play hide and seek?

They are always spotted

** How many times did the other team member laughed, once or twice, add your points!!

Team Mermaid Points: ……../02

Joke Round 15:Team Unicorn:

(It's your turn to read the jokes)

57. What did the candle in the evening?

I am going out tonight

58. Why did the teacher wear sunglasses?

The students were bright

** How many times did the other team member laughed, once or twice, add your points!!

Team Unicorn Points: ..../ 02

Joke Round 15: Team Mermaid:
(It's your turn to read the jokes)

59. Which school does Giraffe go?

High School

60. Which animal can jump higher than the house?

All animals (houses can't jump)

** How many times did the other team member laughed, once or twice, add your points!!

Team Mermaid Points: ..../02

Joke Round 16: Team Unicorn:

(It's your turn to read the jokes)

61. What did the digital clock say to the wall clock?

Look I have no hands

62 What did the triangle say to the circle?

You are pointless

** How many times did the other team member laughed, once or twice, add your points!!

Team Unicorn Points: ……../02

Joke Round 16:Team Mermaid:
(It's your turn to read the jokes)

63. What happens when a snowman bit a dog?

The dog would have a Frostbite

64. This bow cannot be tied?

Rainbow

** How many times did the other team member laughed, once or twice, add your points!!

Team Mermaid Points: ……../02

Joke Round 17:Team Unicorn:

(It's your turn to read the jokes)

65. How to make 7 even?

Take away S(s Even)

66. Why are frogs not good pirates?

They are jumping ships

*** How many times did the other team member laughed, once or twice, add your points!!*

Team Unicorn Points: ……..../02

Joke Round 17:Team Mermaid:
(It's your turn to read the jokes)

67. **Why was 'B' always chilled out?**

It was near AC (A..B..C)

68. **What happens to the old snowman?**

It becomes water

** *How many times did the other team member laughed, once or twice, add your points!!*

Team Mermaid Points: ……../02

Joke Round 18:Team Unicorn:

(It's your turn to read the jokes)

69. Where did the Lizard go after losing its tail?

Re-Tail store

70. Who teaches Math to the Chicken?

Mathemachicken

** *How many times did the other team member laughed, once or twice, add your points!!*

Team Unicorn Points: ……../02

Joke Round 18:Team Mermaid:

(It's your turn to read the jokes)

---

71. How does nut Sneeze?

Cashew

---

72. Why did the pie visit the dentist?

For a filling

** How many times did the other team member laughed, once or twice, add your points!!

Team Mermaid Points: ……../02

Joke Round 19:Team Unicorn:

(It's your turn to read the jokes)

73. Which ring does a burger gift?

Onion Ring

74. What did the cat say to the mouse before the race?

Are you kitten me

** How many times did the other team member laughed, once or twice, add your points!!

Team Unicorn Points: ……../ 02

Joke Round 19: Team Mermaid:

(It's your turn to read the jokes)

75. The dog can stop any video, why?

They have paws (pause)

76. The twin octopus looking similar is called?

I Tenticle

** How many times did the other team member laughed, once or twice, add your points!!

Team Mermaid Points: ……../02

Joke Round 20: Team Unicorn:
(It's your turn to read the jokes)

77. Why was history easy to cave people?

Because there was no historv

78. If you had 2 apples 3 strawberries and a pineapple, what would you have finally?

Fruit Salad

** How many times did the other team member laughed, once or twice, add your points!!

Team Unicorn Points: ……../02

Joke Round 20:Team Mermaid:
(It's your turn to read the jokes)

79. Can the teacher punish you for something you didn't do?

Yes, if you didn't do your homework

80. What does shark says when they do something great?

Jawesome (Awesome)

** How many times did the other team member laughed, once or twice, add your points!!

Team Mermaid Points: ..……../02

Joke Round 21: Team Unicorn:

(It's your turn to read the jokes)

81. What is the name of the person with rubber toe?

Roberto

82. How to party on Mars?

You Planet (Plan it)

** How many times did the other team member laughed, once or twice, add your points!!

Team Unicorn Points: ……../ 02

Joke Round 21: Team Mermaid:
(It's your turn to read the jokes)

83. What is frog's favorite at Mc Donald's?

French Flies

84. Why did the boy throw the butter out of a window?

To see Butterfly

** How many times did the other team member laughed, once or twice, add your points!!

Team Mermaid Points: ……../02

Joke Round 22:Team Unicorn:

(It's your turn to read the jokes)

85. What's the update of the race between lettuce and tomato?

Lettuce was ahead ,but the tomato is trying to catch up (Ketchup)

86. What do Bumble Bees Chew?

Bumble Gum

** How many times did the other team member laughed, once or twice, add your points!!

Team Unicorn Points: ……../02

Joke Round 22:Team Mermaid:
(It's your turn to read the jokes)

87. What time would the monster come to town?

When it is time to run

88. Why did the dog's classmates didn't share secrets with him?

Because the dog was teacher's pet

*** How many times did the other team member laughed, once or twice, add your points!!*

Team Mermaid Points: ……../02

Joke Round 23:Team Unicorn:

(It's your turn to read the jokes)

89. Which school subject has most fruits?

History (Full of dates)

90. Which key opens the banana?

Monkey

** How many times did the other team member laughed, once or twice, add your points!!

Team Unicorn Points: ……../02

Joke Round 23: Team Mermaid:
(It's your turn to read the jokes)

91. How do you get spoiled milk?

From a pampered cow

92. Who makes money driving their customers away?

The Cab Driver

** How many times did the other team member laughed, once or twice, add your points!!

Team Mermaid Points: ..../02

Joke Round 24:Team Unicorn:

(It's your turn to read the jokes)

93. Why is foot very special body part?

It has its own soul

94. Why was the report card wet?

Because it has C (sea) grade

** *How many times did the other team member laughed, once or twice, add your points!!*

Team Unicorn Points: ……../02

Joke Round 24:Team Mermaid:

(It's your turn to read the jokes)

95. How do the Gold Fish ages?

Take out the G (G..old)

96. Where do ghosts live on the road?

At dead ends

** How many times did the other team member laughed, once or twice, add your points!!

Team Mermaid Points: ……../02

Joke Round 25:Team Unicorn:

(It's your turn to read the jokes)

97. Which Key everyone used on Thanksgiving?

Tur key

98. Why did the Teddy Bear didn't eat?

It was stuffed

** How many times did the other team member laughed, once or twice, add your points!!

Team Unicorn Points: ……../02

Joke Round 25:Team Mermaid:

(It's your turn to read the jokes)

99. Which is Polar bear's favorite burger?

Iceberg-er

100. These cattle were humorous?

Laughing Stock

** How many times did the other team member laughed, once or twice, add your points!!

Team Mermaid Points: ……../02

Points Table of Joke Round

(Add up your points and write the total here)

Game 2: Riddle

- Each team would get a Riddle in each round and three attempts to answer correctly.

- If the other team member can solve the Riddle, they get 2 points for every correct answer. If the answer is close and not exact, the team could be given 1 point as decided by the Umpire.

- Add the points at the end of the chapter.

Let's apply the mind and solve the riddles!

Riddle Round 1

1. I can make 2 chocolates out of one?

Mirror

** Did the Team Mermaid answered the correct answer (2 points)or were close (1 point)?

<u>*Team Mermaid Points:* ..../02</u>

Riddle Round 1

2. If you clean me, I become black?

Blackboard

** Did the Team Unicorn answered the correct answer (2 points)or were close (1 point)?

Team Unicorn Points: ……../02

Riddle Round 2

3. The more you take away, the more I become?

Hole

** Did the Team Mermaid answered the correct answer (2 points)or were close (1 point)?

Team Mermaid Points: ..../02

Riddle Round 2

4. I am without wings, legs but can fly?

Smoke

*** Did the Team Unicorn answered the correct answer (2 points)or were close (1 point)?*

Team Unicorn Points: ..../02

Riddle Round 3

5. Do you know of a word that contains all 26 letters?

Alphabet

** *Did the Team Mermaid answered the correct answer (2 points)or were close (1 point)?*

Team Mermaid Points: ……../ 02

Riddle Round 3

Team Mermaid: It's your turn to read the Riddles

6. In a race you pass the person in 2nd position, what's your position?

Second

** Did the Team Unicorn answered the correct answer (2 points)or were close (1 point)?

Team Unicorn Points: ……..../02

Riddle Round 4

Team Unicorn: It's your turn to read the Riddles

7. There was a boat full of people, yet I was unable to see a single person, why?

All were married, no single person

** Did the Team Mermaid answered the correct answer (2 points)or were close (1 point)?

Team Mermaid Points: ..../02

Riddle Round 4

Team Mermaid: It's your turn to read the Riddles

8. How many bricks are required to complete a building?

One (The last one)

** Did the Team Unicorn answered the correct answer (2 points)or were close (1 point)?

Team Unicorn Points: ..../02

Riddle Round 5

9. These 4 days start with letter T?

Tuesday, Thursday, Today, Tomorrow

** *Did the Team Mermaid answered the correct answer (2 points)or were close (1 point)?*

Team Mermaid Points: ……..*/02*

67

Riddle Round 5

Team Mermaid: It's your turn to read the Riddles

10. You would never have these for lunch?

Breakfast and Dinner

** *Did the Team Unicorn answered the correct answer (2 points)or were close (1 point)?*

Team Unicorn Points: ……../02

Riddle Round 6

Team Unicorn: It's your turn to read the Riddles

11. What is moving left to right now as you read?

Your Eyeballs

** *Did the Team Mermaid answered the correct answer (2 points)or were close (1 point)?*

<u>*Team Mermaid Points:*</u> ....*/02*

69

Riddle Round 6

12. Which month has 30 days?

All the months

** *Did the Team Unicorn answered the correct answer (2 points)or were close (1 point)?*

Team Unicorn Points: ..../02

Riddle Round 7

13. Where does yesterday come after Tomorrow?

In the dictionary

** *Did the Team Mermaid answered the correct answer (2 points)or were close (1 point)?*

<u>*Team Mermaid Points:*</u> ..../02

Riddle Round 7

14. What can you only see in the middle of March and April?

R

*** Did the Team Unicorn answered the correct answer (2 points)or were close (1 point)?*

Team Unicorn Points: ..../02

Riddle Round 8

15. You can never see it ,but it is always ahead of you?

Future

** *Did the Team Mermaid answered the correct answer (2 points)or were close (1 point)?*

Team Mermaid Points: ……../02

73

Riddle Round 8

16. Your empty hands can fill it?

Gloves

** Did the Team Unicorn answered the correct answer (2 points)or were close (1 point)?

Team Unicorn Points: ..../02

Riddle Round 9

17. What becomes shorter after adding two letters?

Short

*** Did the Team Mermaid answered the correct answer (2 points)or were close (1 point)?*

Team Mermaid Points: ..../ 02

Riddle Round 9

Team Mermaid: It's your turn to read the Riddles

18. This is made of water and dies in water?

Ice

*** Did the Team Unicorn answered the correct answer (2 points) or were close (1 point)?*

Team Unicorn Points: ..../02

Riddle Round 10

Team Unicorn: It's your turn to read the Riddles

19. In this month people sleep the least?

February (Least number of days)

** *Did the Team Mermaid answered the correct answer (2 points) or were close (1 point)?*

Team Mermaid Points: ……../ 02

Riddle Round 10

20. It goes through water without getting wet?

Light

** Did the Team Unicorn answered the correct answer (2 points)or were close (1 point)?

Team Unicorn Points: ..../02

Points Table of Riddle Round

(Add up your points and write the total here)

Game 3: Who Am I

- Each team would get a Who Am I in each round.

- Three attempts would be given to answer. If it is answered correctly, 2 marks would be awarded.

- If the umpire feels the answer was close, 1 marks would be given.

- Add the points at the end of the chapter.

Let's apply our mind !

Who Am I Round 1

Team Unicorn: It's your turn to read the Riddles

1. I always come to the picnic uninvited?

Ants

** *Did the Team Mermaid answered the correct answer (2 points)or were close (1 point)?*

Team Mermaid Points: ……../02

Who Am I Round 1

2. I am always at the dinner table ,but you can't eat me?

Plates and spoons

** Did the Team Unicorn answered the correct answer (2 points)or were close (1 point)?

Team Unicorn Points: ..../02

Who Am I Round 2

3. You can get into me easily but it's difficult to get out?

Trouble

*** Did the Team Mermaid answered the correct answer (2 points)or were close (1 point)?*

<u>*Team Mermaid Points:*</u> *……../ 02*

Who Am I Round 2

Team Mermaid: It's your turn to read the Riddles

4. You can hear me, control me but can't see me?

Your voice

** *Did the Team Unicorn answered the correct answer (2 points)or were close (1 point)?*

Team Unicorn Points: ……../02

Who Am I Round 3

Team Unicorn: It's your turn to read the Riddles

5. Which letter of the Alphabet has most water?

C (Sea)

** *Did the Team Mermaid answered the correct answer (2 points)or were close (1 point)?*

<u>*Team Mermaid Points:*</u> *……../02*

Who Am I Round 3

Team Mermaid: It's your turn to read the Riddles

6. The more you take me, the more you leave me behind?

Footsteps

** *Did the Team Unicorn answered the correct answer (2 points)or were close (1 point)?*

Team Unicorn Points: ..../02

Who Am I Round 4

Team Unicorn: It's your turn to read the Riddles

7. What belongs to you, but others use it more than you?

Your Name

*** Did the Team Mermaid answered the correct answer (2 points)or were close (1 point)?*

Team Mermaid Points: ..../02

Who Am I Round 4

Team Mermaid: It's your turn to read the Riddles

8. I come once in a minute, twice in a moment but never in a year?

The letter "m"

*** Did the Team Unicorn answered the correct answer (2 points)or were close (1 point)?*

Team Unicorn Points: ..../02

Who Am I Round 5

Team Unicorn: It's your turn to read the Riddles

9. I have hands but can't clap?

Clock

*** Did the Team Mermaid answered the correct answer (2 points)or were close (1 point)?*

Team Mermaid Points: ..../02

Who Am I Round 5

Team Mermaid: It's your turn to read the Riddles

10. I am full of keys and make music?

Piano

** Did the Team Unicorn answered the correct answer (2 points)or were close (1 point)?

Team Unicorn Points: ……..../02

Who Am I Round 6

Team Unicorn: It's your turn to read the Riddles

11. I am very light, but you can't hold me for long?

Breath

** Did the Team Mermaid answered the correct answer (2 points)or were close (1 point)?

<u>*Team Mermaid Points:*</u> ……../02

Who Am I Round 6

12. The more you use it, the sharper it becomes?

Brain

** *Did the Team Unicorn answered the correct answer (2 points)or were close (1 point)?*

Team Unicorn Points: ……..../02

Who Am I Round 7

Team Unicorn: It's your turn to read the Riddles

13. Forwards I am heavy, and backward I am not?

Ton

** *Did the Team Mermaid answered the correct answer (2 points)or were close (1 point)?*

Team Mermaid Points: ..../02

Who Am I Round 7

14. I have many holes but can still hold water?

Sponge

** *Did the Team Unicorn answered the correct answer (2 points)or were close (1 point)?*

Team Unicorn Points: ..../02

Who Am I Round 8

Team Unicorn: It's your turn to read the Riddles

> ## 15. I pop out as the rain comes, who am I?
>
> *Umbrella*

** *Did the Team Mermaid answered the correct answer (2 points)or were close (1 point)?*

Team Mermaid Points: ..../02

Who Am I Round 8

Team Mermaid: It's your turn to read the Riddles

16. I am green and copies others, who am I?

Parrot

** Did the Team Unicorn answered the correct answer (2 points)or were close (1 point)?

<u>*Team Unicorn Points:* ……../02</u>

Who Am I Round 9

Team Unicorn: It's your turn to read the Riddles

17. The more I cry, the more light I create, who am I?

Candle

** *Did the Team Mermaid answered the correct answer (2 points)or were close (1 point)?*

Team Mermaid Points: ..../02

Who Am I Round 9

Team Mermaid: It's your turn to read the Riddles

18. I am hard as a rock and die in water, Who am I?

Ice

** *Did the Team Unicorn answered the correct answer (2 points)or were close (1 point)?*

Team Unicorn Points: ..../02

Who Am I Round 10

Team Unicorn: It's your turn to read the Riddles

19. I am more useful if broken, Who am I?

An Egg

** *Did the Team Mermaid answered the correct answer (2 points)or were close (1 point)?*

Team Mermaid Points: ……../02

Who Am I Round 10

20. It's a shower, but no water is used, Who am I?

Baby Shower (Ask your mommy about your's!)

** Did the Team Unicorn answered the correct answer (2 points)or were close (1 point)?

Team Unicorn Points: ……../02

Points Table of Who Am I Round

(Add up your points and write the total here)

Game 4: Knock Knock Jokes
You Laugh You Lose

- Each team would get one joke at a time.

- If the other team member laughs at the joke, 2 points are given to the first team (team reading the joke).

- Add the points at the end of the chapter.

- Let the Umpire decide in case there is any confusion in whether the other team laughed or not. *(A smile is also considered for a point!)*

Let's start with jokes, control your laughter to win! He He!

Knock Knock Round 1:Team Unicorn:

(It's your turn to read the jokes)

Knock Knock.

Who's There?

Murray.

Murray who?

Murray Christmas to you.

** How many times did the other team member laughed, once or twice, add your points!!

Team Unicorn Points: ……../02

Knock Knock Round 1:Team Mermaid:

(It's your turn to read the jokes)

Knock Knock.

Who's There?

Beehive you.

Beehive who?

Beehive Yourself

** How many times did the other team member laughed, once or twice, add your points!!

Team Mermaid Points: ..../02

Knock Knock Round 2: Team Unicorn:

(It's your turn to read the jokes)

Knock Knock.

Who's There?

Barbie.

Barbie who?

Barbie Q

** How many times did the other team member laughed, once or twice, add your points!!

Team Unicorn Points: ……../ 02

Knock Knock Round 2:Team Mermaid:
(It's your turn to read the jokes)

Knock Knock.

Who's There?

Boo.

Boo who?

Stop crying, I was kidding.

** How many times did the other team member laughed, once or twice, add your points!!

Team Mermaid Points: ……../02

Knock Knock Round 3:Team Unicorn:

(It's your turn to read the jokes)

Knock Knock.

Who's There?

House.

House who?

House about coming out.

** How many times did the other team member laughed, once or twice, add your points!!

Team Unicorn Points: ……../02

Knock Knock Round 3:Team Mermaid:

(It's your turn to read the jokes)

Knock Knock.

Who's There?

Nobel

Nobel who?

Knocking because Nobel

(No Bell)

** How many times did the other team member laughed, once or twice, add your points!!

Team Mermaid Points: ……../02

Points Table of Knock Knock Round

(Add up your points and write the total here)

<u>Total Points</u>

(Add up your points and write the total here)

Joke Round		
Riddle Round		
Who am I Round		
Knock Knock Round		
Total		

<u>My Other Books You Would Enjoy</u>

Just search for Author Natalie Fleming

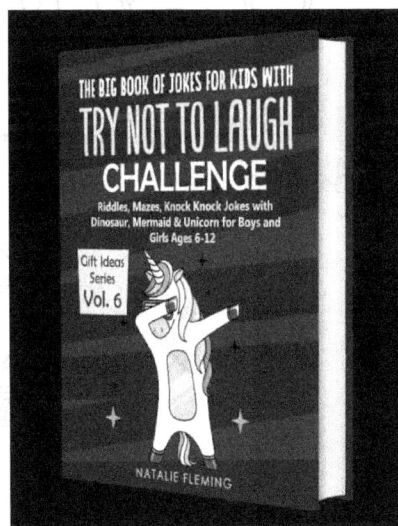

Did the kids enjoy it!

If yes, leave your kind comments and reviews.

For suggestions reach out to us at Valueadd2life@gmail.com

If you want to get Slime Making Recipes and receive updates about our new releases

Either Click Here

Or copy/type

http://eepurl.com/dtOspz

Cheers!

Natalie

Facebook: **@NFlemingauthor**

CPSIA information can be obtained
at www.ICGtesting.com
Printed in the USA
BVHW011959200322
631963BV00018B/185

9 781674 017754